HAUS CURIOSITIES

The Power of Judges

About the Contributors

Claire Foster-Gilbert is the founder director of the Westminster Abbey Institute. A current and former member of numerous ethics committees, Foster-Gilbert has played an instrumental role in the medical research ethics field, and has led efforts to shift the Church's thinking on environmental issues.

David Neuberger was president of the Supreme Court of the United Kingdom from 2012 to 2017. He was elected an honorary fellow of the Royal Society in 2017, and is a member of the Council of Reference of Westminster Abbey Institute.

Peter Riddell is a British journalist and author of many books including *In Defence of Politicians* (2011). He is the former director of the Institute for Government and is now the Commissioner for Public Appointments.

Edited and with an Introduction by Claire Foster-Gilbert

THE POWER OF JUDGES

A dialogue between David Neuberger and Peter Riddell

First published by Haus Publishing in 2018
4 Cinnamon Row
London SW11 3TW
www.hauspublishing.com

Copyright © Westminster Abbey, 2018

The right of the author to be identified as the author
of this work has been asserted in accordance with
the Copyright, Designs and Patents Act 1988

A CIP catalogue record for this book is
available from the British Library

Print ISBN: 978-1-912208-23-4
Ebook ISBN: 978-1-912208-24-1

Typeset in Garamond by MacGuru Ltd

Printed in Spain

Contents

Acknowledgements

Sincere thanks are due to the Dean and Chapter of Westminster, the Council of Reference and Steering Group of Westminster Abbey Institute, Ruth Cairns, Charles Haddon-Cave, Harry Hall, Peter Hennessy, Kathleen James, Igor Judge, Brian Leveson, Seán Moore, Barbara Schwepcke, Jo Stimpson, Sunbeam House in Hastings and Moore's Cottage in Knockanure, County Kerry.

Introduction

In 2015 and 2016, Westminster Abbey Institute held a series of dialogues on the subject of power as it is exercised in the institutions of Government, Parliament, the Judiciary and the media. This little book contains the dialogue between David Neuberger and Peter Riddell on the power of judges. The introduction offers some context for the dialogue, held within the ancient walls of Westminster Abbey on Parliament Square, and attempts an explanation of what can seem a bewilderingly complex legal system – evolved over many centuries – within which our judges operate, including discussion of the implications of Brexit on UK law. It also comments briefly on some of the challenges both of the system and to judges.

Westminster Abbey Institute was created to nurture and revitalise moral and spiritual values in public life and service, through working with people of all faiths and none in, among others, the institutions that sit on the other three sides of Parliament Square: the Legislature in the Houses of Parliament to the east; the Executive in the Treasury and all of Whitehall to the north; and the Judiciary in the Supreme Court to the west. It is rare for the hard-pressed people in these institutions to be given the opportunity to draw breath and recollect what their public service is for, to reconnect with their vocation to public service and the values and virtues that underlie it and to thereby recharge their moral batteries. Westminster Abbey Institute seeks to provide the means for this refreshment of the souls of the people and institutions so engaged. The series of dialogues on the nature of power was offered in this spirit, as is this book.

The UK constitution puts elected political representatives at its heart and this is where, rightly, responsibility finally rests for the laws that are brought into being. But politics means power-seeking, as MPs are obliged to attend to being selected, elected and re-elected, and to positioning themselves within their parties. The volatility that this entails is given considerable stabilising ballast by the constitutional provision of a non-political Executive, including the Civil Service, Armed Forces and Security Services, and a non-political Judiciary. All of these are bound by the constitution to administer, uphold and enforce the laws made by Parliament – ultimately by MPs. And all of these institutions, like MPs themselves, owe loyalty first of all to the Crown, which has no direct power at all. Democracy – the right to elect our leaders – is protected and sustained precisely because it, in all its vulnerability, is supported by people and institutions that do not seek political power. Furthermore, while democratic institutions are of fundamental importance, total concentration of power in any one branch of Government is dangerous and undesirable.

Some might argue that it would be preferable, and certainly

more democratic, to elect our judges, as in the US. Unlike those in the UK, US judges at federal level are nominated by the (democratically elected) President and confirmed in post by the Senate, and at state level are directly elected. But, by being more democratic, the process also removes political independence, a development which David Neuberger would deplore. By contrast, UK judges are appointed. Until the Constitutional Reform Act of 2005, the Lord Chancellor was responsible for appointing judges, who did not need to apply; they were invited. Now the Lord Chancellor is also the Secretary of State for Justice and a Cabinet Minister, and does not even have to be a lawyer. The role of appointing judges has been taken over by the Judicial Appointments Commission, which was created by the 2005 Act. Appointments thus no longer depend upon being known and favoured by one individual, the Lord Chancellor (although in past practice Lord Chancellors generally consulted the most senior judges on their decisions), but are made through a transparent application process. The process is more accountable and accessible, and, as David Neuberger observes, probably inevitable in today's climate. Nevertheless, there is a feeling that something has been lost from a time when those who would become judges did not have to apply for the post.

The law maintains the minimum standards of behaviour required for peaceable living in society. It does so by means of laws themselves and the courts that administer them, by which disputes can be resolved and those who cause harm can be punished.

UK laws include statute law and the common law. Statutes are Acts passed by Parliament, that is to say, by our democratically elected representatives. The common law is laid down by judges, who develop it from precedent (earlier judicial decisions) in areas not covered by statute. Judges also interpret statutes. The judicial role in developing the common law and interpreting statutes allows for flexibility which is beneficial in a world of rapid social, commercial and technological change. An example of such a case is that of Ms B., who had requested to have her life support machine switched off and be allowed to die.[1] The judge in this case had to interpret the law against murder (the deliberate ending of a life) and the law against battery (the treatment of a patient against her express wishes). The judge ruled that Ms B.'s treatment should be allowed to be withdrawn, and the case now sits within the common law and is referred to in similar cases.

The courts which administer the law are several. In England and Wales these are, in increasing seniority: i) in criminal law, the magistrates' courts and the Crown Court; ii) in civil private and public law, the County Court and the High Court, and parallel with them the First-tier Tribunal and the Upper Tribunal; iii) in family law, the magistrates' courts, the County Court and the High Court; iv) above them all, the Court of Appeal; and v) above that, the only UK-wide court, the Supreme Court, of which David Neuberger was president until 2017. Most criminal, civil and family cases begin with the lowest tier of courts, depending upon their seriousness. No cases start in the Court of Appeal or (with the exception of some devolution issues) the Supreme Court: these courts generally only hear cases against which appeals have been made, that is, when the judgements made in lower courts have been challenged. The Supreme Court, which is the final arbiter and hence the most powerful court in the land, conducts its appeals in front of several judges, the Justices of the Supreme Court – normally numbering five but sometimes as many as nine (and on one occasion eleven)[2] – who come to unanimous or majority judgements, and who decide important points of law. Recent judgements have included the ruling that Parliament and not a referendum has the authority to decide that there should be legislation to bring about the departure of the UK from the European Union (EU);[3] the ruling that the Northern Ireland abortion law is an infringement of rights as defined by the European Convention on Human Rights;[4] the ruling that the ban on different-sex couples entering into civil partnerships infringed their rights;[5] and rulings on assisted dying.[6]

Until the UK leaves the EU, all UK courts are bound by decisions of the European Court of Justice in Luxembourg, founded in 1952, which is the supreme court of the EU in matters of EU law. All EU law, while the UK is in the EU, is part of UK law by virtue of the UK's membership. Upon the UK's withdrawal from the EU, the Luxembourg court will no longer have jurisdiction over it, save to the extent that any new agreement between the UK and the EU provides otherwise. Whatever the terms of such an agreement, there are thousands of EU laws that have been passed during the 45 years of UK membership of the EU, and their status has to be decided. To address this question, the European Union (Withdrawal) Act 2018 has prospectively repealed the European Communities Act 1972 and will bring into UK law *all* the EU laws (although this is likely to be qualified by further legislation depending on, and reflecting, any new agreement between the UK and the EU). A lengthy process of sifting has begun, in which laws which are deemed no longer desirable or relevant will be discarded. This complex unravelling of 45 years of shared legislation requires each Government Department to comb through the laws relating to its policy areas – for example, the Department for Environment, Food and Rural Affairs (Defra) is looking at the thousands of laws relating to environmental policy and practice, fishing, farming, other food production and more. In many cases, the changes needed are minor and technical, such as removing obsolete terms like 'EU'. These changes will be made by means of 'secondary legislation' or Statutory Instruments. Statutory Instruments are scrutinised by the House of Lords Secondary Legislation Scrutiny Committee, which hitherto has only very rarely challenged them.

Where the changes to the former EU laws are more substantial – 'substantial' having been defined by the European Union (Withdrawal) Act – a House of Commons 'sifting committee' called the European Statutory Instruments Committee will scrutinise the proposed changes and advise whether they need to be treated as primary legislation and hence be subject to a vote in Parliament. The process is lengthy, cumbersome and, as Hansard Society senior researcher Joel Blackwell has argued, toothless, since the sifting committee can only advise, not enforce.[7]

The UK is also subject to the European Court of Human Rights in Strasbourg, which exists to uphold the European Convention on Human Rights ('the Convention'). This is a treaty obligation arising from the UK's membership of the Council of Europe together with 46 other countries. Under the treaty, the UK must accept those decisions of the Strasbourg court which apply to cases on the Convention arising in the UK or involving a UK citizen. Until 2000, the UK Government's duty to observe the Convention was only effective on the international plane, and it formed no part of domestic UK law – but, in 1998, the Human Rights Act was passed, bringing the Convention into UK law with effect from 2nd October, 2000. The Human Rights Act 1998 requires UK judges to 'have regard to' *all* decisions of the Strasbourg court which are of relevance to the case in front of them. In practice, this means that UK courts will follow the European Convention on Human

Rights, unless to do so would contravene a provision in UK statute law or (as happens from time to time) the UK courts believe that the Strasbourg court has gone wrong and should reconsider its position. Parliament has indicated that, when the UK courts declare that a statute is incompatible with the Convention, Parliament customarily addresses the question of whether that statute should be changed. Almost invariably, the necessary amendment to the statute is passed, not least because the UK accepts that it is bound by treaty obligations. An exception to this, to which David Neuberger refers, was the case on whether prisoners should be deprived of the right to vote. The Convention states this should not happen, and UK statute states it should. (After prolonged consideration and reconsideration in the UK and in Strasbourg between 2005 and 2017, the Lord Chancellor proposed a compromise whereby a very few strictly defined prisoners may be given the vote, which the Strasbourg court accepted.) Peter Riddell and David Neuberger also discuss the implications of the Human Rights Act for UK legislation on assisted dying. Treaty obligations arising from membership of the Council of Europe will continue notwithstanding Brexit. There are no current proposals to repeal the Human Rights Act.

The courts have three distinct areas of responsibility: i) trying those accused of breaking the law (criminal law); ii) resolving disputes between individuals and institutions including companies (private civil and family law); and iii) ensuring that the state and all public bodies act lawfully and protecting citizens from the misuse of power (public law).

In the first area of responsibility, courts which try those accused of breaking the law have a vital role in keeping the peace. Without the assurance that those who are proven to be guilty will be brought to justice, people may take the law into their own hands: for example, there is nothing at which I would stop short to avenge harm done to my own child. In the second area, the courts resolve disputes between individuals – for example, divorce or custody cases, disputes between neighbours or over contracts, or insurance claims. Sometimes these disputes are dealt with by arbitration, which takes place in private and is presided over by an arbitrator (often a senior barrister or retired judge) chosen by the parties to the dispute, but is otherwise much like a court. They can also be resolved by mediation, which (if it works) is a great deal quicker and cheaper. In the third area, the courts address public law issues, including human rights claims and protecting the citizen against the state, normally in the form of judicial review cases. These involve judicial consideration of proposed or actual policies or actions of Ministers, Government Departments, local councils or other public bodies, and can be sought by anyone who believes that a public body has overstepped the boundaries of its power, failed to follow due procedure or contravened the Human Rights Act. David Neuberger and Peter Riddell discuss this function, particularly in the context of increased surveillance in response to terrorist threats and the consequent loss of individual privacy.

There is a very real danger that justice through the courts is, in practice, only available to institutions or the very rich. The law seems opaque and complicated to ordinary people. It is not nearly as diverse as it should be, and judges, like all of us, suffer from unconscious bias. These are problems of which David Neuberger is all too aware. In the dialogue he notes the disadvantages that lack of diversity brings not only to individuals but also to the Judiciary itself, and recalls that, when he was president of the Supreme Court, he ensured its Justices received training against their unconscious bias. The law is also unavailable to ordinary people because it is expensive. As legal aid has been successively cut and become available to fewer people, so access to justice has decreased. David Neuberger and Peter Riddell discuss ways in which access to the Judiciary might be improved: it is unquestionable that more money is needed to assist the delivery of justice, not only by increasing the amount and availability of legal aid, but also by investing in the court system to make it more efficient and effective. As David Neuberger points out, it is neither reasonable nor just to grant by law rights to individuals that they then cannot exercise because of the absence of resources to do so.

There is evidence that judges themselves are suffering from low morale that has continued to worsen over the last few years. Some of this evidence comes from a reduced number of applications from high-calibre candidates to enter the Judiciary. To move from a successful private practice as a barrister or solicitor into the Judiciary is likely to cause a significant reduction in income; the deal that made such a move desirable was that judges received a generous pension, but that is no longer the case. Judges feel they cannot make a public fuss about this because a judge's salary, though lower than those of many barristers or solicitors, is still considerably higher than that commanded by most people, and they would not gain much public sympathy for their plight. Nevertheless, the consequence is that lawyers who would make good judges are not coming forward, unless their call to public service is so great that it overcomes other, more personal, financial concerns. A recent survey of all judges by University College London (UCL), to which David Neuberger refers and to which there was a 91% response rate, showed that serving the public ranks highest in the reasons given to be a judge: 83% said they were judges because it gave them the chance to contribute to justice being done, and 69% did it because it was public service. Nevertheless, the study reported, a large proportion of them would today discourage suitable applicants from applying to be a judge.[8]

The UCL study shows that financial pressures are not the only ones to bring about a crisis in recruitment to the Judiciary. Many judges stated that their job has changed significantly since they were appointed; 73% feel too much of that change has been imposed upon them, and 51% said the change has brought them to breaking point. The drivers for change, 91% believe, are Government policy initiatives (that high percentage no doubt related to the fact that a minuscule 2% of them feel valued by Government). Only 4% feel valued by the media. The lack of support from the Secretary of State for Justice following the *Daily Mail* headline 'Enemies of the People' on 4th November, 2016, with its echoes of Nazi Germany, still resonates throughout the Judiciary as a confirmation of its belief that its role in upholding the constitution and the rule of law is simply not recognised by most of the media and most politicians.

The UK legal system is based upon intelligent and sound principles which have justice at their heart, but it is creaking and in great need of the sort of gentle improvement and reform that the British constitution, at its best, has enacted over hundreds of years. Without this investment, there is a danger that the judicial system will itself come under question, and that more radical solutions will be proposed, such as the introduction of a written constitution – which might make more sense rationally, but would lack the subtleties and creative possibilities that a mature unwritten constitution allows.

Not only the system but also the people who uphold it are in need of attention. To serve the public without fear or favour is a palpable and explicit motivator for the Judiciary. The UCL survey demonstrated it; the Judge's Oath expresses it:

'I... swear by Almighty God [or solemnly affirm] that... I will do right to all manner of people after the laws and usages of this realm, without fear or favour, affection or ill will.' But the will to serve can never be taken for granted, and it may falter under the pitiless gaze of a critical and uncomprehending public. Judges are perhaps the most exposed public servants of all. They cannot hide behind the anonymity of officialdom; they do not share the responsibility for their judgements with others; their judgements are in the public domain and remain so in perpetuity. Judgements are difficult and often highly complex, and they have to be made on a daily basis. They can have enormous, sometimes devastating consequences. Judges, as well as the people they affect, have to live with their decisions for the rest of their lives, and their record stays with them, however much they may wish to forget. For intelligent, thoughtful, empathetic people to be willing to step into the exposed position of judge, a society needs demonstrably to view the position with high regard, understanding better than we do currently the judicial process and the constitutional importance of judicial independence.

The will to serve the public justly and fairly shines through the words of the dialogue partners, as does their belief that judges for the most part fulfil this high calling. David Neuberger's modesty is exemplary. While being realistic about the challenges, then, the dialogue nevertheless offers an inspiring picture of the good that the power of judges can do.

Dialogue

Rt Hon Lord Neuberger, speaker in this dialogue, was the second president of the Supreme Court, which was opened by Her Majesty the Queen in October 2009 to replace the Appellate Committee of the House of Lords. David Neuberger studied Chemistry before working at the merchant bank N. M. Rothschild & Sons from 1970 to 1973, until he entered Lincoln's Inn and was called to the Bar in 1974. He was made a Queen's Counsel (QC) in 1987 and became a bencher for Lincoln's Inn in 1993. His first judicial appointment was as a recorder from 1990 until 1996, when he was appointed a High Court judge in the Chancery Division. He was then the Chancery Supervising Judge for the Midland, Wales and Chester and Western Circuits from 2000 to 2004. In 1999 David chaired the Advisory Committee on the Spoliation of Art (in the Holocaust). Since 2000 he has been a governor of University of the Arts London. In 2003 he became chair of the Schizophrenia Trust, now merged into Mental Health Research UK, of which he is a trustee. He has also led an investigation for the Bar Council into widening access to the barrister profession. In January 2004 Lord Neuberger was appointed a Lord Justice of Appeal. In 2007 he was made a Lord of Appeal in Ordinary and was created a life peer as

Baron Neuberger of Abbotsbury in the County of Dorset. He was appointed Master of the Rolls in 2010 and then returned to the Supreme Court as president in 2012. David has sat as judge in the most senior Hong Kong court, the Court of Final Appeal, since 2010. David is a member of the Council of Reference of Westminster Abbey Institute.

Rt Hon Peter Riddell has been Commissioner for Public Appointments since April 2016, responsible for ensuring that appointments to boards of public bodies are made on merit after fair and open competition. He was formerly director of the Institute for Government from 2012, where he had previously been a senior fellow at the same time as working for the Detainee Inquiry, a Privy Counsellor panel looking at whether the British Government was implicated in the improper treatment of detainees held by other countries. At the Institute, he co-authored reports on transitions and ministerial effectiveness, and was closely involved in its work on political and constitutional reform. Until mid-2010, Peter was a journalist for nearly 40 years, split between the *Financial Times* and *The Times*, at the latter of which he had been a domestic political analyst and commentator. He has been a regular broadcaster, has written seven books and has delivered frequent lectures. He chaired the Hansard Society, a non-partisan charity which promotes understanding of Parliament and representative democracy, for five years until mid-2012. He carried out the triennial review of the Committee on Standards in Public

Life for the Cabinet Office in late 2012. He has received two honorary doctorates of literature, is a fellow of the Royal Historical Society and an honorary fellow of the Political Studies Association, and was one of the first recipients of the President's Medal of the British Academy. He was appointed to the Privy Council in July 2010 in order to serve on the Detainee Inquiry and was made a Commander of the Order of the British Empire (CBE) in the 2012 Birthday Honours List.

The text below is a lightly edited version of the dialogue. Additional comments made by David Neuberger and Peter Riddell to expand points made in the original dialogue are enclosed in [square brackets].

Peter Riddell

The series of dialogues of which this, 'The Power of Judges', is a part, is entitled 'In Power?' I think one of the interesting things which will emerge in our conversation will be: is the word 'power' right? Do people actually have a sense of power? I was pleased to be asked to contribute to this dialogue partly because of my experience as director of the Institute for Government. That institute is on the other side of St James's Park, in another space and geography, and it exists to improve the effectiveness of Government. But when I look at Government, what strikes me is how it sits within different silos. People in British public life belong not to just one establishment, which is the frequent accusation made, but to several establishments, several different power structures, and they don't talk to each other much. At the Institute for Government, as at Westminster Abbey Institute, people are brought together – not in quite the same way, but both institutes make evident that the language spoken by the Judiciary, the Executive, politicians, the clergy and others is different, and the different groups react and behave in different ways.

This wasn't always so. Here we are, in this beautiful chapel built by Henry VII. Henry VII wouldn't have recognised in any respect at all distinctions between, particularly, clergy and lawyers. He wouldn't have had much time for the Commons certainly, and not always for the Lords. He would regard them as all merged together. Indeed, if we go back just 150 years, the Judiciary was sitting in Westminster Hall. It must have been rather noisy with all the courts meeting there. Even in David Neuberger's own period when he was a Law Lord, a member of the Appellate Committee in the House of Lords, he sat in a committee room in the House of Lords. It is less than a decade since the legislation was passed to create the Supreme Court on one side of Parliament Square. So while constitutionally there may have been distinctions between the Judiciary and the Legislature, the physical proximity was very strong. Not that long ago, members of the Supreme Court would have given rulings upstairs in a committee room in the Lords in the morning, and in the afternoon spoken on and moved amendments downstairs in the Chamber of the Lords, against the

Government of the day. That memorably happened. A lot of the contradictions within the legal system surfaced there, in the Lords.

Today, I'm delighted to introduce David Neuberger, whose career is as an extremely distinguished judge. He was a member of the Appellate Committee when it was sitting over the road in Parliament, on the east side of Parliament Square, before it was replaced by the Supreme Court, on the west side of Parliament Square. Then he became Master of the Rolls and then president of the Supreme Court. He has always been interested in the wider aspects of the Judiciary, diversity and its relationship to the wider citizenship. And those are among the concepts I want to explore.

[First, David, you have filled the highest office a lawyer can achieve. Would you tell us something of your journey to that place – what your ambitions were, what you hoped to achieve, why it was your choice of career?

David Neuberger

As your introductory words revealed, I came to the law relatively late – a scientist at University, and banking for my first, inglorious, career. After two years as a banker, I realised it was not for me, and, after casting around for inspiration and discussing possible careers with friends in other jobs, I decided I wanted to be a barrister. I suppose it was a case of rejecting all other possibilities. I opened my first law book more or less on my 25th birthday, and discovered I did indeed enjoy it. I think I had never considered it because my mother, quite an influence in my life, did not approve of lawyers. She never really liked me being a barrister, and was delighted when I became a judge. After passing my Bar exams, I had to find a set of chambers, initially as a pupil (that is, a trainee) and then as a tenant (that is, a practising barrister). These days, pupillage is relatively difficult to get, but, once you get it, you have a good chance of a tenancy; in those days, gaining a pupillage was relatively easy, but it was harder to graduate into a tenancy. That is because pupils must now be paid, but that only started happening in the 1980s. I did three successive pupillages in different chambers, at the end of which each of the chambers chose someone other than me as a new tenant. I almost gave up in despair, but I allowed myself one last chance in what were then significantly less prestigious chambers than the three I had failed to get into, and they specialised in landlord and tenant law, which did not greatly attract me. It turned out to be the opposite of 'beware what you wish for': in terms of both work and colleagues, the chambers suited me extremely well. I managed to build up a successful practice, becoming a QC after twelve years or so, and then I was offered a High Court judgeship. For almost all my time at the Bar I had never dreamt that one day I would become a High Court judge; no one in our chambers ever had. I felt very honoured to be appointed. And thereafter I was in the right place at the right time, and managed to clamber all the way up the judicial ladder. I am not being falsely modest. Of course, you are more likely to succeed if you are intelligent, hard-working, committed, honest, sensible and friendly, but, for better or worse, luck plays an enormous part in our personal and professional lives, and I was very lucky. As a senior judge, I didn't have great plans; I have always believed that little, unspectacular changes are best. Of course, there are times when big changes are called for, but I think people in charge are too readily attracted to radical changes – it makes them feel important, and we are very good at seeing all the disadvantages of the present system while being blind to the disadvantages which will flow from its replacement. After around 40 years in the law, I have come to realise that one of the few laws which is consistently reliable is the law of unintended consequences.]

Peter Riddell

What of the concept of justice? When we go into the Supreme Court building, we are struck by grand statements about justice, about being the pinnacle of the judicial system. But is it quite like that? I'm not quite being Dickensian and evoking the spirit of *Bleak House* and the fog and so forth, but it can appear remote from ordinary people, can't it?

David Neuberger

I think that traditionally it has been seen as important that the law is somewhat remote, somewhat detached, somewhat to be feared. That is partly because justice has always to be detached, almost Olympian. Judges famously take an oath to dispense justice without fear, favour, affection or ill will: these are human features, emotions, which we have to forswear. But it's partly also to make people respect the law, and to make people more likely to tell the truth, and to behave properly in the face of the court. I think those are all still relevant functions and features, but in the 21st century we are more conscious of the need to ensure that people understand what is going on in court – both the general public and individual litigants and witnesses. Over the past few decades we have attempted to take the law to the non-lawyers and explain to them what's going on in individual cases. We have tried to explain to witnesses what is going on; to take away much of the Latin, many of the technical expressions; and, so far as the public is concerned, to try to explain to them what we are doing and why. In the Supreme Court, for example, we've taken advantage of its relatively new creation to stream what is going on, so you can watch us hearing cases. We are also filmed summarising our judgements in short and simple terms, and we produce longer written summaries, so that the public and journalists can quickly understand them rather than having to read sometimes 100 pages of our judgements. We are physically more easily accessible to the public than we were in the House of Lords. All those features are, I think, important. It's easier for the Supreme Court than for most other courts: we are adequately funded, and we don't have to worry about witnesses, let alone juries, being intimidated or nervous because they're being filmed. And when it comes to visitors, we don't have to worry about people losing their way and not knowing where they are; we have relatively few courts and we are relatively prominent and easy to find.

Peter Riddell

But there is a sense, isn't there, of a caste apart, in the same way that the priesthood is a caste apart, and often politicians too? You appear different from ordinary people in one obvious way: that the senior Judiciary is still dominated by men of a certain background.

David Neuberger

Yes, first of all there is a necessary element of detachment. You talked earlier about the silo effect of the Judiciary, the Executive and the Legislature. I remember when I was at the House of Lords, members of the House of Commons who ceased being MPs and became Peers said how little they knew about the House of Lords until they got there. So even between the Houses of Parliament there's less intercommunication than there should be. Separation of powers does not mean that we should not talk to and understand each other: on the contrary, we should. Nonetheless, I think that the judges have to be detached to some extent in that we can't express views about a number of issues in public because that's not our function. We also have to be detached because as judges we have to decide cases without any appearance of bias and without any actual bias.

The issue of diversity is another matter, and it is important. For the Judiciary in the past, fewer than 50 years ago, there were no women or non-white senior judges at all. Things have got better in the past 50 years, but particularly among the senior Judiciary we have quite a way to go still. I think it's particularly important among the Judiciary that we become more diverse. First, it is inevitable that if you choose from a smaller pool you are going to get fewer excellent people, and giving up the opportunity of getting some of the best people is worse than unfortunate for the Judiciary. Second, for a profession primarily concerned with justice it is plainly unfair that we should have an unjustifiable overrepresentation of one group. Third, there is a risk of the public losing confidence in a Judiciary which is not representative and fairly selected. And fourth, when deciding cases it is important for judges to bring to the table – or, rather, the bench – as many different views as possible, as many different experiences as possible. And that is only achievable if you have a properly diverse Judiciary.

Peter Riddell

Another aspect where people think the law is remote is that

no ordinary person would want to bring a case because of the cost of it, the time involved in it. It is curious to think, when we see the wonderful new court, the Rolls Building in Fetter Lane, that it is heavily populated by oligarchs suing each other. The law is one of our great exports, and it's a badge of honour for Britain that people want to bring their legal cases here because they respect British justice and British lawyers: they want to have their commercial cases done here. This clearly brings a lot of money to Britain and employs a lot of people. But if it is inaccessible to ordinary Britons because of the cost, is justice being done?

David Neuberger

When one says there are two legal professions, people normally think you mean barristers and solicitors, but in a way there are two legal professions in a different and more worrying sense. Those who advise and act for large organisations, rich individuals, large companies, Government Departments and so on are well paid, sometimes very well paid, and have clients for whom costs are not normally the primary concern. Not only do these lawyers earn a very nice living, they perform a very important role, particularly in this country where we are so dependent on what used to be called invisible earnings and are now I think called the service industries. As several Lord Mayors of London (and not just lawyer Lord Mayors) have made clear, the legal profession in this country provides a very important role in the service industry. First, London is one of the top legal advice and dispute resolution centres in the world; indeed, many people think that it is *the* top centre. Second, a strong legal system with outstanding lawyers and judges supports all the other service industries: it is very difficult to have a thriving banking system or insurance market without a strong legal system to back it up. And it is therefore important for the economy. That side of our legal world is fine, although like many people I wonder if it is at risk of pricing itself out of the market: even the very rich have their sticking points.

Where there are bigger problems is amongst the lawyers who represent ordinary people. Legal aid was available for a large number of people until about 1999, but from then on this aid has become harder to get and less available, and this has meant that it has become more difficult for ordinary people to litigate. This is worrying, particularly if it gets worse, because it is wrong to give people rights (whether they are human rights or rights against your neighbour, your spouse or somebody who knocks you over) if they can't actually enforce their rights – and the only respectable method of enforcement is, of course, by going to court. Similarly, if you are sued by somebody rich, you must have the opportunity to defend yourself.

Now, lawyers are very good at blaming the Government and saying that they have to provide more money. The lawyers are not wrong; the Government should provide more money.

But one appreciates that there are problems for the Government at the moment: money is limited. And I think the lawyers and judges have a duty too. We have to make the cost of litigation, and the time it takes, proportionate. It is ridiculous that we have a system where if somebody has a claim for £20,000 it would cost that person and his or her opponent each, or even between them, £150,000 to fight. Where we can, we have to make it proportionate. Easy to say, of course, not so easy to do.

Peter Riddell
Isn't that an argument for almost a parallel system, using mediation or arbitration much more, where the costs can be less and the time can be less too? There's a distinction between arbitration and mediation, of course.

David Neuberger
Yes, arbitration is basically private litigation. And I don't think it really saves much money. You have to pay your arbitrator and you have to pay for your room, etc, so it often costs more. But you are quite right that mediation can reduce costs and increase accessibility. Mediation involves the two sides in a dispute getting together informally with a third party, a mediator, who tries to encourage and shepherd them into making a settlement. It's terrific if it works: it is much quicker and cheaper than litigation and, equally importantly, much

less stressful because it brings about a solution to the case in a relatively amicable way. But, of course, you can't make people settle, and if the mediation doesn't work it has added to the cost, added to the time and probably added to the bad feeling. The figures that I've seen suggest that, in most cases where it is tried, mediation works, and I think that the general perception is that in the great majority of cases, big and small, mediation should be encouraged.

Peter Riddell

The law has historically always been underpinned by religion in various ways. Indeed, in many countries with different faiths there's still a very strong underpinning. How do you see the interlinking of religion and the law today?

David Neuberger

I think, as you say, in the past they were very closely linked together. Famously, in 1676, the Chief Justice Sir Matthew Hale said that 'the Christian religion is a part of the law itself'.[9] But in 1883 the Lord Chief Justice at the time, Lord Coleridge, said it was 'no longer true... that Christianity is part of the law of the land',[10] and I think many people nowadays would say that religion and law were unrelated. I personally consider that the position is more nuanced than that. In the end, both religion and law are trying to achieve justice, fairness and morality. They are both based ultimately on what we think is right. But they are not perfect. Religion does things occasionally which aren't right; the law produces results in individual cases that aren't morally right, at least in most people's eyes.

But take very basic rules. For instance, in court, witnesses are expected to tell the truth: that's morality. The law of contract is that people should keep their word: that's morality. The sermon in Westminster Abbey marking the beginning of the legal year this year [2015] was on the story of the Good Samaritan. That story has the Old and New Testament injunction to 'love your neighbour as yourself'. The law, with its slightly less emotional and more dry view of life, transposes that into saying you should refrain from performing actions or making omissions which may be reasonably expected to harm your neighbour. It's a bit more of a mouthful and a bit less engaging, but it is saying the same thing. So I think there are similarities between law and religion, and they can learn from each other, but they are a good deal further apart than they were perceived to be 400 years ago.

Peter Riddell
Even further back, Magna Carta directly linked law and religion at the time – issues like usury and so on.

David Neuberger
Oh yes. As you say, there is overlap between lawyers and the

church, as well as the establishment more widely. After all, our courts are called courts because originally we were the king's judges or queen's judges and we operated in the king's court. The idea of separation of powers was unknown, and at least that situation had the advantage, I suppose, of not having the silos in which we all now work.

Peter Riddell

Indeed. Some of the disputes leading up to the murder of Thomas Becket were conflicts of jurisdiction between the church courts and the royal courts – particularly over taxes – and, in a forerunner of the much later arguments in the Reformation era, between papal and national claims to sovereignty.

Turning to the question of the nature of judges' power, what would you say about the role of judges in making and interpreting the law? Traditionally, judges would be responsible not for making law but for interpreting it. More recently you have been charged with judicial activism: you are making the law, not just interpreting it any longer. The balance has changed.

David Neuberger

It has always been the case that judges have made the law to some extent, but the basic truth is that if Parliament legislates for something in a statute it's not open to the judges to make law inconsistent with that. Judges have to apply statutes. Although the UK has three branches of Government – Parliament, the

Executive and the Judiciary – what Parliament says ultimately goes. It's true that judges have become more, if you like, proactive over the past 50 years, and particularly the past 20. However, that is largely because Parliament has conferred those powers on us, and the fact remains that if we do something Parliament doesn't like, if we make a decision Parliament doesn't like, Parliament can overrule us. So the idea of the unelected judges overruling or contradicting the elected members of the House of Commons is false, because even if we decide that a statute means what Parliament didn't intend it to mean, which does happen, Parliament can always change the law.

Peter Riddell
What about the areas where Parliament hasn't taken a view? During the 1970s, Parliament took a view on some of the really big moral issues such as homosexuality, abortion and divorce. In a sense, those new statutes made it less hard – if I may put it that way – for the courts, because they were clear. That is no longer necessarily true. The classic issue that exemplifies this lack of clarity is assisted dying, on which the House of Commons recently rejected any change in the law. In the Supreme Court you had already seen cases coming up on this issue, and it is likely that there will be more. Doesn't this put the courts in a position where you start to look as though you are challenging Parliament, because Parliament has declined to take a view?

David Neuberger

Probably the biggest factor in increasing judicial power, or at least the perception that judicial power has increased, has been the Human Rights Act 1998. The Suicide Act 1961 says that assisting a suicide under any circumstances is a crime. Now, if that's what statute says, even if you passionately believe it is wrong, as a judge you have to accept that it is the law. However, by enacting the Human Rights Act, Parliament has decided that the judges can rule that a particular statute conflicts with human rights in some way or another and make a declaration accordingly. The issue we had in the Nicklinson assisted suicide case was whether the Suicide Act, legalising suicide but prohibiting in all circumstances assisting a suicide, conflicted with the rights of people who were incapable of killing themselves but, because they felt their lives were useless, wanted to be assisted to die.[11] We couldn't say helping them was legal, because Parliament had said in the Suicide Act that it was illegal. But we could have said, and what two of the nine of us did say, was that the Act conflicted with the European Convention on Human Rights, enshrined in the Human Rights Act – that is, the human rights of those people who wanted to kill themselves or be assisted to die. We didn't decide that the Suicide Act conflicted with human rights, but if we had it would still have been open to Parliament under our system to say, 'Thank you very much, judges, that's what you think, but we're not going to change the Suicide Act or make a new law.'

Up to now, save in relation to prisoners' votes, Parliament has always taken our judgement on board when we've said that a particular statute conflicts in some way with human rights, and has amended the law, effectively in favour of the Human Rights Act. But under our constitutional system Parliament has the last word, and it's up to Parliament what happens.

One of the effects of the Human Rights Act, together with the way that administrative law has moved – that is, judges considering, through judicial review, how local authorities, Ministers and other branches of Government have carried out their functions – is that we have become, if you like, more political, or at least more involved in policy-making. It may be a good thing, it may be a bad thing, but it is what has happened. However, the safety valve in our democratic system is that Parliament has the last word.

Peter Riddell

Yes, with one important caveat: Europe. I don't mean the European Court of Human Rights in Strasbourg, I mean the EU, because once we accepted entry we accepted under the Treaty of Accession the superiority of European law.

David Neuberger

That is true, but the judges in this country only accept that European law trumps Parliament because Parliament has said so in a statute – that is, the European Communities Act 1972.

As Parliament has repealed the European Communities Act with the European Union (Withdrawal) Act 2018, we are no longer able to trump Parliament through the EU. It always comes back to Parliament's decision.

[Peter Riddell

When the possibility of Brexit first arose, I remember considerable apprehension among the senior Judiciary about the scale and unpredictability of the impact. Now that we are in the middle, both of the negotiations with Brussels and of the passage of several bills through Parliament, how do you see the legal implications of Brexit?

David Neuberger

Even in 2018, more than two years after we voted to leave, we are in as much of a state of uncertainty as we ever were. I am afraid I can only say 'wait and see'.

Peter Riddell

How have developments following the EU referendum affected the balance between the Judiciary and Parliament, particularly the judgements over the winter of 2016–17 that only Parliament – and not just the people in the June 2016 referendum – could vote to trigger the process of exiting from the EU? These rulings led, of course, to the lurid charge in the *Daily Mail* that the judges were pro-EU and 'enemies of the people'. How do you counter the charges of 'the judges versus the people'?

David Neuberger

The notion of 'the judges versus the people' is, depending on one's mood, farcical absurdity or insidious nonsense. Parliament decided to have the referendum, Parliament decided that it would not be binding. The judges were merely interpreting the law that Parliament had made, and were doing so in accordance with the rule of law. That's our job. We would be letting down the people if we did not decide cases according to the law. There are times when I think we pay a heavy price for freedom of expression. But some things never change. Stanley Baldwin, Prime Minister in the 1930s, referred to the press having power without responsibility, which he described as 'the prerogative of the harlot throughout the ages'.[12]]

Peter Riddell

The issue of becoming more involved in political decisions also covers a couple of other points related to the balance between the citizen and the state. Particularly if we have long periods of one party in Government, we see an increase in judicial reviews of policy; we saw this in the long period of Conservative rule between 1979 and 1997. The increase in judicial reviews may also reflect a new generation of younger judges, of which you were one coming up at that stage—

David Neuberger

I was!

Peter Riddell

—and this is perhaps a response to the political circumstances. Do people look to the courts to offer some sort of counterbalance if there is a long period where one party is in power?

David Neuberger

I think they do. Put simply, the courts have three important functions. The first is the one everybody knows about, which is to ensure that the people who are accused of crimes are fairly tried and dealt with according to the law. The second is to resolve disputes between individuals, whether between neighbours or married couples – that is, private rights. And the third, which you're focussing on, is to protect the citizen against the state, to ensure that when a citizen considers that their rights have been infringed in some way by the state – a minister or a local authority or some other organisation – they have the opportunity to come to court, and the function of the judges is to say, 'Yes, your rights are being infringed,' or, 'No, they're not.'

Peter Riddell

The era of mass terrorism produces other conflicts that are judicial too, in particular those that lie between the state's wish to protect its citizens and the human rights of those citizens.

David Neuberger

That is perfectly true. Legal problems often involve balancing two competing interests or two competing arguments. Sometimes the arguments relate to each other, but very often they are more like ships that pass in the night. The threat from international terrorism on the one hand and personal liberty from the state on the other hand have nothing much in common. They're both very important. Balancing them, for a judge, indeed for anybody, is remarkably difficult. It's one of those areas where it is particularly important to ensure that, although as judges we have to be independent, we do have some degree of contact with the law-makers, with the Executive, with the Security Services and with groups representing individuals' rights, so that we understand what's going on.

Peter Riddell

Isn't that difficult to achieve?

David Neuberger

One has to do it in a way which preserves our, and their, independence. But at least we have to understand each other.

Peter Riddell

The Constitutional Reform Act 2005, which created the Supreme Court, also created the Judicial Appointments Commission. We now have judicial machinery which is more independent of Ministers – though not totally independent – to appoint judges. I'd say it is classically British, and in contrast to what happens in other systems. In the US, judges are elected to the Supreme Court. I vividly remember going to a fundraiser for the equivalent election at state level in Austin, Texas. Judges were raising money from tort lawyers who had appeared before them earlier that day and would be appearing before them the next day. Now, I'm certainly not advocating that, but inevitably there are going to be questions about judicial appointments if judges become more involved in the political process.

David Neuberger

Yes, I think that's true. I wouldn't for a moment favour the US system of potential judges for the Supreme Court being called before a Parliamentary Committee to be approved. I think that would be destructive, and watching what happens in the US is not a good advertisement for it. Nor would I favour judges being elected, as many US state judges are.

We have had very good Lord Chancellors taking great care over appointments, but I suppose the previous system wouldn't have the public confidence that an organisation like the Judicial Appointments Commission has. The Commission consists of some judges and some other lawyers, but a majority of laypeople, and they can be much more open – both as to what they're doing and as to how they do it. And, although it means we have a more expensive system, and it can take longer and it is not so comfortable for judges who want a promotion, or those who want to become judges, I think that it's not so much a good thing as an inevitable thing.

Peter Riddell

This greater formality is true of other aspects of British public life now. If you go back to when you trained as a lawyer there was much more informality generally in the working of British public life. It was the 'good chaps know best' view of things, and it was found in the Civil Service and in politics as well as the law. Now, British public life is increasingly codified and statutory. We don't have a written constitution in the sense that Germany or the US has – indeed, all but three or four countries in the world have written constitutions – but we do have statutes which have a constitutional bearing. Does that change the role of the Supreme Court and the Judiciary as a whole? Are you being dragged in much more to some big constitutional questions because there are now statutes? For example, it's already happening on devolution. [And the Supreme Court has been pulled into deciding on the balance of powers between Westminster and the devolved legislatures over Brexit.]

David Neuberger

The most obvious constitutional function we have is in

relation to devolution, and maybe Brexit, although the Miller case may be a one-off.[13] On devolution, if there's an argument about whether the Scottish Parliament or the (Welsh) National Assembly or the Northern Ireland Assembly has the right to do something, or the power to do something, we decide that as the Supreme Court.

The European Convention on Human Rights could be said to be something like a constitution, but the truth is that we don't really have what I would regard as a constitution. In my view, a constitution involves a coherent document (expressed in great detail in places like Germany, in much less detail in places like the US), which basically purports to set out how the country is run, and normally can't just be reversed by a simple majority in Parliament. We have nothing like that at all. People like to think that the Magna Carta or the Bill of Rights is a constitutional document, but almost all of Magna Carta – 58 of its 61 clauses – has simply been repealed by Parliament. To be fair, many of them have been re-enacted in fresh statutes, but they are then no different in practice from any other statute. To that extent, together with only Israel and New Zealand, we are one of the very, very few democratic countries which don't have a formal constitution. There's a debate in many quarters between those who think we should have one and those who think we shouldn't, and it's quite a difficult debate. On the one hand, we have managed as a country pretty well without one for a long time, but on the other, as our system becomes increasingly complicated and there are more complaints about different aspects of it and uncertainties, there's an argument for at least investigating quite carefully whether we should have a constitution. Personally, I would be very cautious about creating one.

Peter Riddell

But in practice the UK Supreme Court is becoming more of a constitutional court, though not in the same way as the US Supreme Court. We don't have some of the unfavourable effects of the US approach where nomination hearings become intensely politicised – a massive political battle. But in practice you may be pulled in the constitutional direction as we have more devolution legislation and bills going through Parliament, now with substantial effect. That is likely to result in more cases which go up through the Appeals Court to the Supreme Court, so de facto you may become more like that.

David Neuberger

The British approach seems to involve sleepwalking into a system by means of a change here and a change there in response to a crisis, or because it seems a good idea. But it would be quite difficult for us to develop into a constitutional court like the German or American ones without a positive and conscious decision to restructure our system significantly. I've been emphasising the fact that we can't overrule

Parliament, whereas the US Supreme Court and the German Supreme Court can say, 'Sorry, you may have passed this piece of legislation, Parliament, but we're afraid it's unconstitutional and we are going to quash it.' For the UK, that would mean unelected judges could overrule Parliament.

Peter Riddell

Finally, how robust is the judicial system as a whole? How confident do you feel, given all the pressures which you face and you've described – the constitutional challenges, the problems of access to the legal system, legal aid and so on?

David Neuberger

There are a number of potential problems. First, we have a problem with our lack of diversity, both in public perception and also in reality. I hope and believe this is being addressed. Second, in England and Wales, the court system is groaning and in danger of collapse. We need a serious injection of money, which is being considered, and a serious rationalisation of the courts and of the technology available to us, so that the courts system really is fit for the 21st century. Third, specifically for the Judiciary, I think that there is a problem at the moment, as the recent survey conducted with the assistance of UCL shows that judicial morale is quite low.[14] That is partly, I think, attributable to the way the court system runs and the amount of work that is required of judges, which could be helped, if not solved, if the whole system were more effective and more efficient. But frankly, there is a related problem about money. Whether you like it or not, many of the best lawyers whom we would like to appoint as judges practise at the commercial end of the Bar, where they make quite a lot of money, and they have to be prepared to take a large cut in pay to become judges. That has always been a bit of a problem, but I think there is a risk now that the recent changes in legislation mean that we could have a very serious problem about recruiting good people in the way we have in the past. It's a difficult story to tell, because, by most people's standards, judges are paid very well. But as is often said by Government Ministers, when they want to say it, you have to pay the rate for the job.

Peter Riddell

This has been an absolutely fascinating discussion. Thank you, David Neuberger, for your candour.

David Neuberger

Thank you, Peter. If I have said things that I shouldn't have said, that is due to your charm. If I haven't said anything I shouldn't have said, then I thank you for encouraging my discretion.

Notes

1 Ms B. v An NHS Hospital Trust (2002).
2 R (on the application of Miller and another) (Respondents) v Secretary of State for Exiting the European Union (Appellant) (24th January 2017).
3 Ibid.
4 R (on the application of A. and B.) (Appellants) v Secretary of State for Health (Respondent) (14th June 2017).
5 R (on the application of Steinfeld and Keidan) (Appellants) v Secretary of State for International Development (in substitution for the Home Secretary and the Education Secretary) (Respondent) (27th June 2018).
6 For example, see R (on the application of Nicklinson and another) (Appellants) v Ministry of Justice (Respondent) (25th June 2014).
7 Joel Blackwell, 'EU (Withdrawal) Act SIs: will sifting make a difference?', *Hansard Society*, 11th July 2018, https://www.hansardsociety.org.uk/blog/eu-withdrawal-act-sis-will-sifting-make-a-difference (accessed 26th September 2018).

8   Cheryl Thomas, *2014 Judicial Attitude Survey: Report of findings covering salaried judges in England & Wales courts and UK Tribunals* (London, UCL Judicial Institute, 4th February 2015).

9   Rex v Taylor (1676).

10 Rex v Ramsey and Foote (1883).

11 R v Ministry of Justice, op. cit.

12 Stanley Baldwin, speech, 17th March 1931.

13 R v Secretary of State for Exiting the European Union, op. cit.

14 Thomas, op. cit.

HAUS CURIOSITIES

Inspired by the topical pamphlets of the interwar years, as well as by Einstein's advice to 'never lose a holy curiosity', the series presents short works of opinion and analysis by notable figures. Under the guidance of the series editor, Peter Hennessy, Haus Curiosities have been published since 2014.

Welcoming contributions from a diverse pool of authors, the series aims to reinstate the concise and incisive booklet as a powerful strand of politico-literary life, amplifying the voices of those who have something urgent to say about a topical theme.

'Nifty little essays – the thinking person's commuting read'
– *The Independent*

ALSO IN THIS SERIES

Westminster Abbey Institute

The Power of Judges is published in partnership with Westminster Abbey Institute. Westminster Abbey Institute was established in 2013 to nurture and revitalise moral and spiritual values in public life, inspire the vocation to public service in those working in Westminster and Whitehall, identify and defend what is morally healthy in their institutions and promote wider understanding of public service. The Institute draws on Westminster Abbey's resources of spirituality and scholarship, rooted in its Christian tradition and long history as a place of quiet reflection on Parliament Square.

ALSO IN THIS SERIES